WALKING TOWARDS THE SUN

LETTER TO A CHILD DOWN

Elisabetta Turano

www.elisabettaturano.it
www.coriandolino.it

"Mika... He was the one to make me understand that nothing is normal. You will often hear that this one or that one is a normal day: I can't stand this sentence, because all days are different.... And even more foolish than talking about normal days, is defining normal a boy or a girl: these are the banalities we say when we don't want to know other people better."

(J. Gaarder)

A dream. Maybe an utopia or a beautiful fairytale without connections with the real world. This is the first idea that, maybe, you can have during a first reading of the book. Actually I believe that the text should be read thinking of a prospective, of a goal to reach. It's true that many of the topics discussed aren't completely realistic. But it's also true that, if in the last years a long road has been traveled regarding acceptance and education of differently abled, it has been possible only thanks to who has been able of thinking big, watching reality with the eyes of trust rather than with those of pessimism. That confidence that too much often is missing even in who is involved in education because it happens more and more frequently that the urge of framing people in "this" or "that" category, makes losing sight of the individuality of each one with its specificities and potentialities.

So the text should be read in the view of a "pedagogy of hope", the one of who is constantly pointed towards the future and of who has the courage to recognize that the good expectations have the power to make others able to tend to a constant evolution.

Only with these premises, each one of us will be really able to be the leading role of the changing and be able to take someone by the hand and together start "walking towards the sun".

Alessandra Saita.

PREMISE

I want to dedicate this book to the little FILIPPO, that I met when he was 6 month old in his endless tenderness. I thank his parents, for the life and the precious care that they give him day by day in the name of divine and unconditioned love.

Filippo, as all the other children in the world, has the right to live, grow up and dream… And in this book I am dreaming with him.

I want to remember to everyone that our value doesn't depend on the applause of the world: in general who knows all the answers never asked himself a lot of questions. Life is not life if it isn't experienced in the originality of the own feeling.

Each one of us was born to be the unique flower in the garden, unique tree in the boulevard, unique seagull in his freedom.

When I met the little Filippo, I thought that the down syndrome is a cleverness that us mere mortals can't understand.

The way to know the sunlight is only one: it is the

one that connect us to infinity despite the limits of the life itself.

Fondly,

Elisabetta Turano.

THE TREASURE OF LIFE

Between dreams hidden in the heart
And deserts furrowed by dunes
You spot the footsteps traced
by the treasure of life.
If you find rough stones
Melt them with the light of the crystals
As the laugh
When it joins the cry
To celebrate the dance of your heart.
If you meet the emptiness
Brush it, to elevate yourself...
As the wind
When it whispers between the deepest depths
To then erect his hiss
To the highest peaks.
When you meet the darkness
Wait the dawn of the new day
That will turn her back
Even to the densest darkness
In order to fill with new promises
The trunk of your life.

THE MEETING

I can see you little Filippo, in the rays of the sun that are lighting up your journey, in the heart of the people who love you and accept your sweet innocence. I listen to you when, with your naïve recall, you want to tell me something, but you are still too little to talk. Think, you are less than one year old and already conquered the caress of who, like you, knows how to love life in her divine creation.

And if you were never born... how could I be joyful caressing your choppy hands, your soft puppy face and notice the joy of living, in your bright eyes? You are a new gift from God, you are the tender bud that is hatching to cheer up our timeless garden.

You are tiny, but when you look around, you can already easily find who sees you in your brightness of a child, in your tenderness that wants to be accepted without reservations. You are like the rainbow: your colours are soft and brush hope, the joy in growing up and going on.

You listen while you can be silent, you listen the message of the caresses, the sound of words and silences.

You are a child, you aren't a "different". You are a revelation of the one thousand faces of the world and life.

You are a God's son and his presence in your life will win the fragile bars to make you erect your home on an unshakable rock.

The journey of life isn't the same for all of us, but it wants to lead everyone at the same goal: live.

We and you will be walking towards the Sun.

You can't be a "different", because you are similar to everything that the Lord created in order to give birth, and make survive and live the earth: the leaves of the trees and their naked logs, the waves of the sea and the deserts of sand, the clear skies and the heavy clouds, meadows of fresh flowers and rocks covered with bushes.

In the world of nature, infallible laws exist: let's try to observe the presence of a dry leaf in a garden of fresh flowers: isn't it the same dry leaf that, back to the ground, will transform in a new life?

And velvety petals of fragrant roses, as the days pass by, don't turn into the crunch of leaves lived by now?

Does someone think you will may be forced to survive for your particularity? No, you live.

You feed yourself with sensations that not everybody knows, but can only imagine. Or maybe not.

TO THE PARENTS

Mother, I appreciate you for how you have been able to send away from the baby son of god's cradle the egoism of have procreated. And you know that you won't be able to control his life, actually you can't control even yours. You know that your son is a gift, he's not a game or an instrument of your blind passion, your son is a branch of your log but he stretch out towards a new growth.

 If you wouldn't have accepted him, your treasure would tacitly tell you: "I feel how you keep the distance from me when you don't approve me because I am not as you would me to be. You desired me, were you waiting for me to cheer up the world with my birth or because could I become an instrument in your hands?

And if I seemed an ugly duckling to you? Oh no, perhaps it wouldn't be the principle of my life but the start of your tragedy, of an endless conflict between your feelings that swing in the drama between love and rejection, bravery and helplessness. Maybe you would destroy me and make me go back in the dark. But, then, you would regret it, feeling defeated twice and maybe even cruel. Don't do it, I was born from you, but I am son of God. You will find out why I was born. The Lord doesn't want to see his creatures lost. Why was I born? We will find out this together during our journey.

And you father, you're great in accepting Filippo who cheers up not only you but everyone who will be able to recognize him in his innocence, in his greatness of a baby, who is able to make the adults (grown-up?) rediscover the beauty of life. You know that the progress has cancelled the heavy primitive difficulties, but has also created weak souls, inclined to take off every day for the most unthinkable destinations but ready to fall down facing the courage of living. Souls chasing around in an endless race the goals of wellness and they run the risk of never ever meeting up. You know that our eyes aren't always able to see the hidden dangers protected by the shifty glory, the ephemeral joy of possession, the indifference, the praise of the absolute efficiency, the sunset of the simple joy.

At what aim are they putting us near to? Perhaps at the one of consume everything too quickly, even love? No, love has not confines. If you give, without expecting anything, you will receive everything.

AND I SEE YOU LIKE THIS

 Slowly you will start to take your first steps in the world, little Filippo. And I see you toddle on the floor, while you try to run, or when you caress the grass between the meadows, or when your chubby hands play with water on the seashore.

Someone look at you and smiles, tries to play with you and right away becomes your friend because you know how to be joyful.

And they are astonished with you when you find a shell on the sand, or when you are amazed looking at the greatness of the sea.

You are a child who wants to live, play, grow up.

You are loved by all the people who have you close to their hearts, you are able to pass on the happiness that not everybody knows because they aren't able to find the hidden richness in the simple things of life.

You are devoted, you want to donate to everybody your caresses, you want to piffle and spread in the air the harmony for who is sad and thoughtful. And meanwhile the light of life smiles to you.

You are a child who is growing up and it's wonderful watching you growing up. You will play with your friends, listening to the music and getting carried away by her waves of energy that will lead you to dance with harmony. You are calm when you turn yourself to others, quietly you are good in putting attention at what surrounds you, especially if you will meet people disposed to listen your hidden voices and respect your learning rhythms. You will be surer and surer about yourself if others will make you feel that way, bringing out your successes and the little steps that slowly will make great your journey. All the children are like you: all of them want to be understood and gratified, they don't grow up peacefully if they live with feelings of mistrust. For everybody, self-esteem is an important incentive to show the hidden lights and reach the best results.

You will learn how to express your words and discover numbers, imitate the ones who are near you, cooperate and play with them. You will impersonate even the adults and their professions: the musician, the hairstylist, the singer.

You will be really good in communicate using your smile and your facial expressions, with singular words or with short sentences. You will become more and more independent, you will be able to wash up and dress up on your own. You are able to draw the attentions of adults and children because of your enviable sweetness, your sympathy.

It's a joy to watch you growing up and finding out that you are a child like the others. If somebody judges you as a "different" the problem is his, not yours. It doesn't exist only what is visible at the gaze: there is an hidden world, high-spirited, real in every one of us that anybody knows. It's a world made of sensations that seems the light colours of the dawn when its rising when the world still sleeping.

You are happy, authentic and cheerful. If

sometimes you get mad, I hope you will meet who is able to understand you, as I wish this to all the children in the world who need to be welcomed and understood. And most of all accepted for who they are, not according to our models and stereotypes.

You will be an artist and, like all the artists, you will see the world with different eyes.
You are the poetry, the music, the colours, while you make us discover your inner world.

You are a hidden treasure, sweet Filippo: only who learns the way to reach you will be really able to discover and love you more and more. In your trunk you guard precious gems, some of them are known, others are less known. The most unknown are the truest pearls because belong to you and no one else, to your uniqueness of human being. No one of us can resemble to you and you will not be able to resemble to anybody, because each one of us is different from the others.

You are the rainbow that cheers up the sky after the storm, because you are able to go behind the clouds so you can look like the sunlight. That sun that is waiting for you to remind you that you were born to make us discover the greatness of an unlimited mind, without prejudices.

You are free because you don't live between judgments and prejudices, you never want to judge others, you welcome them without reservations. Unfortunately, our mind is often blurred by limited and heavy visions like the frightful clouds that blur the clear sky. Yes, prejudices are clouds able to hide the sun of the life. On the other hand, you are reaching his rays, with your joy of living and the help of your loved ones. Day by day, you are heading towards the sunlight.

Meanwhile you are growing up and you are following your path, the one that God gave you. You like to play with colours: perhaps you will become a painter, who will have fun capturing the oddest shades of the world.

You exist and point yourself out for everything you are able to create with the colours of your fantasy, your energy materialize in a painting, in a song or in a wonderful dance. A dance that reminds us all the harmony and spontaneity of life. Many don't care of guarding the treasures that everyone can find inside of themselves, you do.

You are joyful at every manifestation of love, light and poetry. You are able to transform in a show every manifestation of your joy, cheering up who is around you.

When you will go to school, you will pass your time with the company of your friends and with them you will live the experiences of a path that will lead you to "grow up".

What does it mean, for every one of us, "grow up"? It means have the possibilities to manifest our uniqueness, try to cultivate as far as possible the most beautiful dreams in order to beautify even the world with our creations.

If we don't meet who help us to fulfill and express ourselves, our spirit and our flairs will be mortified. The conventional models haven't been able to give birth or make come to life any creativity come to life.

You are unique: you will learn to read and following your rhythms, meanwhile others will learn from you the joy of living. When you were little you gave answers with your smiles, your vocalizing, you offered your toys, you caressed with your hands all that intrigued you; you played with a lot of objects mimicking and working together with your older friends.

You start to talk, while before you could communicate not with words but even with smiles. Slowly you have become more and more autonomous and your walking towards the sun. You will meet people who will make you gain and regain your self-esteem, during each growth experience. And if someone isn't able to do this, you will give him a beautiful smile: even his skeptical face will light up.

You want to draw a face, a human being and you are worried, don't you know how to do it? Draw slowly a circle, that will become the face, with eyes, nose, mouth. You can even draw a full body, with legs and arms. You will learn to count, till three, five, ten... Words and numbers progress and, like all the children, you will learn to speak according to your experiences and their reworking. You will meet who will be able to make you use actively the language of sounds in order to get you near the abstract concepts.

The meeting with the world of art will allow you to come into contact with sides of your personality that silently exist in your chest. In this way you will be able to express your creativity, free from judges and prejudices and from the sifts that cut the verbal language, and like a lot of other children you will learn that your creative production transform in a mark that lasts in time and in your inner world.

Many times, from difficult, even extreme, situations, it is possible to find unexpected solutions. Thank to diligence and help of who can share, with the people involved, experiences and feelings ignoring prejudices, mistrust and obstacles.

Always look towards the future with renovated trust, welcome every source of inspiration and love, as everyone of us should do. In life, there can be moments in which tragedies and losses will lead us towards delusion and bitterness. But a lot of different ways to face these experiences exist: often challenges and adversities can be transformed in victories.

You will not be like a lot of people who don't love the image of themselves, because you will meet who will know how to make you love yourself. Yes, a lot of people can't find the best way to see themselves and their opinion on themselves. This is the reason of their unhappiness: they grow up afflicted by a series of complex, sometimes of physical nature such as "my nose is too long", "I'm ugly" or "I'm too old". These limits born come from our life experiences, usually from our childhood, when we don't know who we are or

25

what we are or what we should be, but we learn from those who surround us, those who are older and wiser than us and that should love us. If they tell us "you are lazy" "you are stupid "... you will convince yourself you are exactly like that.

True love, for its nature, tends to infinity, in an expansion that doesn't know boundaries, doesn't persuade to stay closed in the exaggerated egoism that leads us to love things in a distorted way, neither let us stay closed in the small circle like in a narrow prison. Even sentimentalism is a distortion of true love.

The true essence of Love surrounds everything in a shining light that has one thousand shades and nuances, it's a vibration that gives joy at the vibration of the soul.

Unfortunately, love is ignored when there are a lot of barriers that divide men the ones from the others: property, race, nationality, social categories, ideologies. The inner urges of the human being are of different natures. There is the urge coming from the better side that leads to help the other brother, the one in need; while the worse side bring us to feelings and actions of indifference or cynicism. We can't judge, because our judgment elements are still limited and narrow.

No one will be able to judge you, my sweet Filippo because you can be like a little sun that brings light and warm, because you are made in the image of God.

Only the skeptic won't be able to see your light, because he tries to always turn his back to the sun and can't see his glow that light up everything.

Instead you will always look up and turn to God. You will turn away your look from the human miseries, trying to walk the streets of perfection and you will feel united with the infinite light from which all the life comes.

THE AUTONOMY

We become autonomous. Every human being must be led to depend on others as little as possible, to manage money, to go out on the area with the use of public transport. There will be who will also help you in this path, getting you used to communicate and promote the ability of inquire, explain what you want in shops and offices. You will be able to reach your habitual places on your own, recognize roads and bus stops, you will check your watch in order to be in time for your appointments. Maybe your growth will be obstructed by some innate difficulties, or maybe by attitudes of fear and ambivalence that can be found in the surrounding environment. Who doesn't believe that, even if in uncomfortable situations, we can reach the autonomy, is afraid. Those who want to have at all costs a protective and caring attitude about you. Those who want to reward you with so much affection and excessive attentions to the point of never letting you free. And when you will go near teenage hood, like all the other guys you will try to detach yourself from your parents, you want to begin your own path.

Today for you, exist some associations that will help you find out what you need to go through your everyday life, your job and your free time.

You are happy, when you find out you have become and adult too, you feel grown up, you feel protagonist when they help you to share growth experiences with your peers, when you manage to overcome several difficulties. You will feel encouraged to go on, you want to grow up more and more when you find out you are confident about yourself. I hope you will find educators and adults in general who know how to address to you with a language appropriated to your sensibility, with proposals that can stimulate you to have more initiatives and courage to do things.

You will be happy to take a small steps at a time, to cooperate with your friends.

As for each one of us, for you it's important to dedicate yourself to the activities that attract you more, that are easily realizable: learning while strengthening your self-esteem. For each one of us, it's important to discover and use our resources, in order to be able to start every path, even the one of operators themselves' creativity.

You, as any other human being, follow the pleasure of knowledge, it's important to meet who will help you cultivate your curiosity so that your mind is always busy and active and projected towards the future, when you will find out the joy of working and producing. Meanwhile you will also find out the beauty of friendship and solidarity, so that you will never feel left alone.

You will abandon the pessimism that is the gloomy view of life: the sun, even behind the clouds, release his irradiation on the earth.

On the paths that we walk through, a lot of times we cry and tears fall down in the dust of life but they don't camouflage with it: they shine and mark a sparkling contrail behind our footprints . Only in the cosmic view we will be able to see the greatness and preciousness of human affairs. We aren't just our bodies, beyond the physical existence, the truest part of us lives.

THE JOY OF LIVING

"I want to spread these seeds

in the arid lands,

where someday will bright

the nobility of my hands.

The sun will listen to my words

and to the suffering thoughts

it will give rich soil to the barest poor.

The sun has saw my eyes

and a white eagle will carry my song

between the throbs of the world.

And I will go on spreading

these seeds

till I will see no more

barren lands around me."

To know the joy of living, first of all it's important not to trust others in building up or finding the image of ourselves. Judgments come from thoughts. Your thoughts are beautiful, so they will make you know what others (with their negative thoughts) can't see.

To help any person who is in a difficult situation it's very important spread images and thoughts of health, wealth, vitality.

Each one of us start walking towards the sun with the help of good will, we try to clear out our minds from false suggestions, from falsified ideas. When I think of you, I see you young, winning, joyful, always surrounded by the light. No, never ever give up, you have to fight against every disease: face it! You don't have to feel alone and abandoned, you are part of the universe and you are invested by a vital stream, which goal is to preserve life, always ready to show up.

Nothing can make us stop existing, dying is rebirth. Death doesn't exist.

Love thoughts are like contrails that start from us

to reach all the people we want to help.

In general, when we come closer to someone, we see a soul. What appears to our eyes has a limited valor: the visual meeting is just an illusion, we mustn't be fooled by it. We try to feel the other's soul. All the people who will come close to you, my sweet Filippo, will not be able to help but find the presence of the divine sparkle in your sweetness. You are a sparkle of the same sun that surrounds who stand in front of you, even if upholstered in a different way. Each one of us is wrong when wants to judge the other too fast: the elements that we base our judgment on are only the exterior ones, while the true ones slip out from us because belong to an higher level of life. Let's leave to the events of life their "going", moved by a divine force that operates from thousands ages, before that our little strength was able to do the little that it is able to do. You, my little big hero, will walk confident through the roads of the world because you father and your mother will be able to give to you their faithful thoughts, because from the highest levels of the

36

Great Life they receive as much high inspirations. They know the life of serenity, they are able to live in a wisely and detached from any pettiness of everyday life.

The vibrations of the Divine Sparkle can be better heard when our thoughts are raised towards the High.

We are soak in the Universal Soul that makes us participants of the feeling of everybody else and in this union each one of us can cultivate his diversity. Each one is a part of a unique life. According to the old wisdom, all the things that exist form just one unit. Love is able to forget all that appears divided. And you will be like the sun, my nice Filippo, because you are able to irradiate from yourself a beautiful light. Everything lighted up by you will be the joy, the freedom, the life.

That's the beauty of life: banal things and important things don't exist, all that exists is important. Live the thrill of the moment, don't wait for the great events that when they happen we don't have even time to brush them. Yes, they slip away fast in the air. How many times do we give up in admiring the greatness of a sunset in order to run behind fantasies that need years of effort and then they are founded on the sand instead that on the rocks? The little things make life great. Do you see? The colours of life are never clear and defined, there are different shades that often our eye can't perceive, because it gets the white just as the white and the black like so it is. But it isn't exactly like this, there is always a little bit of black in the white and a little bit of white in the black.

Be like the train of life, when it crosses its rails to reach the huge lands. I give you the joy of living while you, my sweet Filippo, are dreaming a big tree that hugs the earth with his roots and caresses the sky with his branches. A little tree has been planted in a green plain, you will grow up with it that will grow with you, to realize your dreams. Yes, you will be grown-up too and will brush that piece of infinity like the tree does.

THE HELP

There are moments in our life in which everything seems to fall apart. The sun seems to become darker in our path. Things lose their colour and we feel a sentiment of abandon. But it isn't so, no labyrinth will be without the exit. Never demoralize, my sweet angel, there will always be a new dawn for you. Don't feel mad , don't get closer to sadness when you aren't able to be fast in your quotidian activities and games, you are able to go slowly. In life the failure is as important as the success. The day and the night, the four seasons are necessary for the earth and for the life. You can't develop if you get everything right away. Of course you would come in contact with a crystal existence, but without making steps ahead. Who loves you, will be able to feel himself in you, only the egoistic will make himself the center of the universe, he doesn't understand that your good his also his good and not the opposite. Egoism is keeping for ourselves all that has been received from the other, but you are altruistic and will be able to attract who will give you his help in loneliness moments.

You will never be alone, today there are a lots of paths of solidarity and of love. There are volunteer associations that care about families with children with down syndrome in their difficult educational role and in improving the quality of life of their creatures. Who works in these associations, in fact, tries to actively involve the families and tries to build for each one of them, since the first years of life, a common growth project.

The main purpose wants to be the one of develop the potentialities with the building of individualized operational measures because each one of us is the unique flower of the garden. In this way we will be able to promote an efficient placement in school, in society and in employment.

This work will be coordinated by the help of psychologists, educationalists, speech therapists, teachers, music therapists.

You could enjoy yourself taking part in theater and computer science workshops, in creative manipulations or interesting nights out. Even parents will have the possibility to meet up and discuss and chat about eventual difficulties. These are never lacking in our lives. But I'm sure that you will be able to overcome everything successfully and you mother will be able to say that she has lived the phases of your growth with great satisfaction and surprise. Yes, just like some children's mothers who remember their sons' many positive experiences: one thousand meeting up with schoolmates filled with smiles, words, phrases, books, poems, posters that have marked their children's life.

The attitude of trust that surrounds the families and their creatures can't be repaid with anything and nothing. Thanks to the sensibility of educators, you will be able to live school as an important opportunity of growth, a place in which activities will be thought and structured with attention and enthusiasm. For you, the environments will be cozy; schoolmates will be friends with whom play, learn and compare yourself with serenity. In this way you will learn to have trust in the future, to always desire new experiences, to get near at the creation of a real integration in the various moments of your scholastic and working life. I hope you will always meet adults able to accept and welcome you in your uniqueness, as it should be for every child. Each one of us is unique tree in the boulevard.

The gifts of life always deserve to be accepted, they always want us to discover the one thousand faces of the world.

Some time ago, I met a girl with down syndrome's mother, she told me that in general you feel a big fear, a strong emotion when you become parent of a son with disabilities. She kept telling me that what you immediately feel is fear, a big fear, you feel almost guilty: strong and disoriented moods, that at the beginning are barely recognized by who feels them. A sense of guilt because a son different from how the world would have wanted him has been brought to life, a son different from the expectations of most. Then, slowly you come closer to a new vision of these circumstances: you bravery search significant relationships, wanting to create a true, real, strong space for your son, a space that's able to contribute at the affirmation of a spot of dignity and satisfaction in life. Only cultivating the value for your uniqueness, of your peculiar beauty, of your unmistakable existence, each one of us can think of finding a proper place in life and in society.

Each one of us is unique seagull in his freedom.

YOU ARE UNIQUE

I would recognize, after one thousand years, in the memories of my mind, your silent face and your puffy body caressed by the throbs of life. In addition to a great sweetness, you have aroused in me the desire of knowing you more and more in order to find the infinity resources of your little hands and sweet heart. You were able to capture the attention of who saw you even just for a couple of seconds. You are a special child because you are surrounded by the colour of love. Without words, you told already a lot of fairy tales at who was able to listen to you, you revealed yourself in your capacity of colour even the grey life of who has closed himself in the cages of life or in golden jails.

Yes, only who is prisoner can't find the precious pearl that there is in you. But you are unaware of all of this, you know how to live in freedom, accepting the caresses that you like, listening to the songs that attract you, smiling back at who is able to come near you with the passionate caresses of the heart. I saw you again when you were already grown up and wanted to talk to me, turning to me with gestures, facial expressions, simple expressions of your voice. You wanted to surround yourself with tenderness, love and light. And you already know how to give us a lot of jolliness, with your disarming simplicity that is typical of all the children, but that I see in you in a particular way. You are a lucky child, because your parents have always accepted and desired you in the splendour of your uniqueness. They are glad to have a so special child. I am sure you will always cheer up them with your good mood, your wisdom of the naivety, that entrust itself to the fascinating path of life.

You see, your whispers are pages of life for me, pages that you are writing to cheer up the fading ink of our mind when it run behind crystallized footprints. Meanwhile, you are the joy that reinvents itself, that grows like green grass in the meadows during the spring, leaving the sun and the wind able to caress it. You are not afraid, the others are: Those who live in the dark of the clouds and can't see the clear sky that you are painting. You are majestic in your sweet simplicity because you are able to make us understand the many known streets, the unusual paths that hide priceless treasures. You want to play with the surprises of the life, accepting in yourself every little challenge. You want to live playing with your fantasy, chasing the horizons that we don't know. You are like a ruby between the diamonds, a stone that shine to give its light to the mystery, to make special, like you are, even those who are able to appreciate you. Everything will be fulfilled in the right moment of our life and you are arrived to write important pages in the history of the universe.

You know Filippo, you are and will be a great friend that will always be able to give us a ride when we are crossing the ocean of the life. You are free, because you make your heart dance even when you pick up crumbs, even when you receive the simplest and poorest gifts. You will be wise: who is faithful to the little things of life, will be faithful even to the big ones. Perhaps the world isn't bespoke for you, but you will be able to be bespoke for the world. I hope that many will understand this.

You will be able to accept yourself with your successes, but even with your weaknesses, your failures, without follow unreachable horizons.

We are new in every moment, like everything is new in the world of nature: we are sons of the Sun.

It's difficult to accept our life, our individuality when we meet the risk of adapting excessively to others' opinions, but we still be like the peach blossoms in the spring that can't wait to shine in their florescence. True love has no limits or possession, it hasn't either belonging. In the world, each one of us has his role. True love, the one that never cheats us is the one that unites us with the universe, it's a pure love and it doesn't risk to get ill from selfishness, loneliness, missed voices.

I hope you will always be able to listen to the whispers of the heart, the rest counts for little or nothing at all. There are a lot of people who would like to change their nature, still unaware of the fact that we are like the buds: everyone waits for his florescence. And all the flowers are beautiful and important because they colour the meadows of the world.

LIGHT HAS UNLIMITED SIDES

The big light has unlimited sides. Who wants to help others, sometimes, is mocked by those who still live in the dark of egoism because they are afraid of light.

Often, the fear of getting ill his more dangerous and debilitating than illness itself. Fear itself is a disease that is transmitted not by a virus, but by one man to another. Often, in this way, we turn out to submerge even hope, to exaggerate the problems and destroy our capacity of judgment.

In the complexity of life, a simple answer for each problem can't exist...

Fear is like the night: a shadow that seems infinite and long shadows can be found everywhere. Fear has often altered and destroyed the woven of family and social lives, but if the shadow can be brought to light, it can be fought. Parents are always busy fighting the dangers that can hit their children. Meanwhile, children learn from every mistake: all the physical and emotive experiences create a big and strong effect on a child's memory.

Adults' attitudes and models represent a model that the child always tries to follow. Before they will be able to give it to their sons, parents will have to find the idea of liberty in themselves.

A lot of dreads break up spontaneously if they are faced with bravery.

Fear and anxiety, also, can't be measured: a problem that can be insignificant for someone, turns out to be really serious for someone else.

Spread in the childhood, the seeds of fear grow up in the adolescence till they plant themselves in the adulthood and become obstacles that influence every moment of our life. Instead we try to hug the joy of living, our life and ourselves, accepting us for what we are. You see, the seagull can't fly off like an heron, and yet his flight is still very graceful and showy as the heron's one is. When the moon is on her growing or waning phase, it will not be able to light up the sky with its silver sphere as it does in the full moon phase, but it cheers up with its glowing the dark of the night.

Fear grows and develops in the shadow, but it loses every force when it is submitted to the light of the attention and comprehension.

LIFE NEVER RUNS OUT OF HOPE

Life includes, in addiction to all the manifestations of the senses, also infinite sides that the man can't perceive, the invisibles worlds that slip out at the sensory experience. It is right there that life lives and vibrates in the most sublime way, crossing the human noise in order to be able to listen the silence of the sky.

Our knowledge is limited, but our possibility to know is limitless.

There can't be life without a bond that connects the near to the far, the little to the big, the strong to the weak.

Every manifestation of the nature is a message from the infinite, of which goals are always elevated above the individual's interest. The human goals aren't like these. The man mainly searches his advantage in everything. You child, on the other hand, will love the nature: the sea, the land, the woods, the mountains, the charm of the flowers that are its and your smile.

When children are surrounded by the familiar environment of love end sense of safety, they are able not only to accept and tolerate difficult situations but also to use them constructively. The emotional stability faces the attacks of the fear. We have the duty and the child the need that his sense of safety will be preserved in all his emotional experiences, simple and complex. Remember that children can understand a lot of reasons even if they aren't able to express them. Generally, children have less fears when they are treated patiently and gently and when their personality is completely respected.

"Inclemency melt
like nothing
in the nothing.
Rumbles fall silent
and fireworks disappear.
No noise
will ever scratch
the unspoken voice
of my hope."

We don't need to be frightened to be together .

Let's leave the old patterns behind, so that we can introduce the new ones in our life. Let the fear go away so that we can feel safe. Let's free ourselves from the belief that everything that is new or unfamiliar can make us lose control or make us experiment the danger at any moment.

Instead we know that the biggest contribution that can be done to life isn't made of thoughts and words filled of fear but it is made of thoughts and actions soaked with love. We are also living in an era of hopes and conquests. Scientific researches, helped by new technical and social researches, make us able to destroy once for all our anxieties and worries. Fear, on the other hand, destroys our potential capacities and doesn't allow us to develop intellectually.

EVEN FOR YOU IT WILL BE THIS WAY

Live in the pursuit of the light, even the most hidden one.

Evil or imperfection are not the final truth. Our life is like a river with his banks that seems to imprison it, meanwhile life keeps running between those banks. We reach freedom when we arrive at the development of the truest nature, like the artist when he achieves the artistic freedom getting rid of the temptations of popularity. The beauty of a poem, in order to keep to the rules, goes beyond them.

In order to be really fulfilled we must imitate the waves of the sea: each one rises to his height. Everything that exists could not exist in a different way. Even the most beautiful flower that spreads all around himself his perfume, is forced to fatigue under the sun, the rain, the wind.

THE OTHERS

How the people who surround us see our problems?

Unfortunately we tend to ask advices to others hoping to find comfort and explanations, without realizing that we often have the answer inside of ourselves. All of us would like to be loved and appreciated by others, but we risk to live in depending on this, in order to be able to show our value. Everybody have slants on us, starting from our parents and friends. We could say that everybody have in their mind plans for us, regarding how we should act, behave, think.

But we are not that plan. If we don't agree with another person's bad judgment on us, the problem is of the other person who seems to not understand.

Her judgment does not take anything away from our qualities. Our routine, pattern of thought (and so also prejudices and preconceptions) if on a side create a sort of self-confidence, on the other side can be dangerous for us and other people.

Thinking in a negative way is a widespread habit perhaps now more than ever. A part of responsibility about this is up to the mass media that exalt bad news. Speaking and thinking negatively, inevitably induce to negativity. Sometimes, we express negative thoughts believing we are realistic. So, what could be love for others, if we aren't able to love ourselves first? It's beautiful to think that we accept ourselves for what we are, aware that we will change for the best. Conditions change, even our knowledge does.

THE CREATIVITY

Creative activities are the biggest supporters of positive thoughts and favorite them in the most difficult situations. Singing, playing instruments, drawing something you like, writing a poem or a tale are beauties, very stimulant games for the joy of living. Creativity isn't the opposite of rationality. The most logical inventions would have never existed without intelligence and creativity. Creativity is nothing but the rejection of the spirit to let itself be configured and compressed by strict rules.

And you, my great artist, can express yourself by using paper, pencil and crayons in order to show your freedom following the spirit that doesn't need demonstrations. The intelligence is only mind, the spirit is all the being.

Music is the true realization of beauty because it expresses what any word could not reveal. Music makes us go near the discovery of the infinite, the happiness, the peace. It's a speechless feeling that makes us live like in a spring morning and in its shades and beauties and that transmits us the true sense of life. Music is the melody of the heart throbs, it's the emotion that carries us in unknown worlds, it's a limitless feeling, where conflicts conciliate, where sadness and happiness join together in the beauty of this art form that in every moment brings a message of eternity. In this atmosphere, the unformed can assume a form: of a flower, of a fruit, of a heart. In music the heart shows itself immediately and doesn't have to suffer the obstacle of any barrier, it's never forced to have a meaning like words do. Music is a caress that arrives from the heart of the world directly to our heart.

And you child, you will listen to the music of the world and will dance in the infinite of life.

Like the river can become the sea, so you will become ocean in your simple humility. You are true, you don't have limits because you can't judge other people, even if others can have prejudices about you.

We have been accustomed since our childhood not

to trust our instincts and to believe only in what others say (the adults in this case).

Intuition is something that can't be taught. Rarely, instead, what could be taught is taught, that is hand down to the little children self-confidence, offering them a guide so that they can find their potentialities. Often we end up saying: "But nobody does that way…" even when we have a genial intuition. "it doesn't work, otherwise someone would have done this already, no one does so" meanwhile our intuition is ignored.

"I faced

the greatness of the sea

caressing

his little waves

one by one.

Since then

the unknown

doesn't frighten me. "

WE ARE UNIQUE WITH THE INFINITE

Sank into time and space, we are unique with the infinite. Outside the cage of the limited physical senses in which man is forced to live, we can listen the voice of the soul that guides us in times of uncertainty and doubt. Why staying alone in agony? None of us is ever alone. In the becoming of life is nice to make progress every day, get something new as for all growth. Your progress will be safe, even if you do not notice right away.

You will play, but will not fight against others.

You have to fight only to send away fear from yourself.

You will participate only for fun at races or competitions: run away from what moves in your spirit feelings of rivalry, strife, what brings resentment. Completion leads to fight against others. It is an evil that creates other evils. And you, on the other hand, will try to not harm anyone: you are good and happy to be this way.

You leave to everyone the freedom to watch life

from the point of view that they want, even if in this vision there are shadows and disharmonies. Sons of the same Father, we are different in a temporary "difference" : we are different on the outside, but we are sons of the same sun.

The uniqueness of his rays gives light to every corner of the earth. Like every human being has characteristics that make him unique: this is his richness, our richness.

Unfortunately the biological diversity creates an hostility represented by prejudice that gives rise to attitudes of discrimination and racism: the fear towards the different. Diversity is a richness, not an obstacle.

It's important to create a community like an "us" because the differences are what render the world an interesting place in which live. An innate potentiality exists in each person, in every assignment, in every problem to be faced.

One of the most difficult things to accept is our diversity: The more we accept our diversity, the more we accept the one of others. Feeling far away from the majority is cause of loss, especially during teenage hood. That's why it is important to research and esteem our truth, the only way to understand the sense of our life.

The different isn't the same as you, doesn't think as you do. The different is someone special.

Each one of us, in order to be able to face the wonderful adventure that life is, must feel to be worth it, must be able to do. Self-esteem is like water for the waves of the sea, without it the difficulties of life would be insuperable and worry to be wrong would always born in us. I would like to pray you and all the children to not identify the failure with the sense of your worth.

Since children, we are told that who does wrong is not good, that everything must be well made otherwise you are lower than those who can do better. But the sense of our worth doesn't depend on the applauses of the world and above all doesn't coincide with not being able to do something well. A failure doesn't mean that we are losers, it's just a failure. There is nothing wrong when we are unable to do something. Please, when the dust of defeat wants to wrap your eyes up, don't let your soul be blurred! Don't give importance to those who want to devalue you, those who blame you aren't able to understand, forgive them. They are not aware of what they do. The sense of beauty and of good lives on another planet, lives in our being as manifestations of the divine creation. Nevertheless, we are human beings, we are not God, we can be wrong and have doubts and worries. In life there's always to choose, even if it is not simple to do so. Having doubts is natural even if we would rather never have them, actually it would be great to decide right away and for the best. In the material life doesn't exist any guarantee, true safety consist in don't needing guarantees. Only one thing is sure for me, while I look at you and admire you… your parents have decided the most beautiful thing for you: to give you the life.

Harmony in the world is born when we are able

to communicate, in order to be able to clearly manifest our needs, while from the bottom of our consciousness rise the most authentic states of mind, the true self. Slowly we reach a fantastic, wonderful, out of place and time, out of how and why dimension: the dimension of being. These are the most magical moments, in which we find our essence and we are joyful about it. Communication is to be able to make feel the other what we feel and feel what the other feels. And I wish you to always meet people who knows how to understand your desires and find out your potential talent, someone who can involve himself completely with you, when you want to do and undo, make mistakes and make them again, win and lose, laugh and cry. When we cry because roses become thorns, when services don't function as good as they should and when a lot of people make us angry. We live in a society based on profit and personal advantage, sometimes on exploitation. We can help each other only if we are able to communicate, to ask hoping in solidarity and not in cynicism.

Only in this way we can elevate our soul above

the universal loneliness.

SUNFLOWERS FIELDS

A lot of kids like you are happy to be here, they can have a lot of problems but are able to ride over them, if they find a welcoming environment that will be able to help them. A new generation is conducting them in their growth. A better and more human world is waiting for us.

Emotional relationships are more satisfying and vivifying the more they are true, even when the viewpoints are different, because it's exactly in how the difficulty is dealt together with the truth that we can measure a group's creation. Of course, we always fatigue in accepting what's different from us, even through the dialogue between ourselves and interlocutors you can understand that there are not many aspects in common, this is a skill that can be acquired only by focusing our attention on what we like of the other person.

The different is a voice, a soul. The issue of "diversity" for culture, origin, capacity is always dark and meanwhile fascinating. And it arouses contrasting feelings: rejection, fear, mystery. So a boundary where the different can be beautiful and original, or misguided and destroyed, is created. Even the different for geniality, risks to sacrifice his own destiny in the name of a presumed normality, that becomes backbreaking for him. No one likes to be considered racist, but racism exists, sometimes even against ourselves when it's difficult to accept our peculiarities or when our resources aren't understood. But who knows all the answers, generally, has never asked himself a lot of questions. To overcome the limits of our thoughts, we have to think in a new way, focusing our attention on the lights and the flashes, without being frightened of the shadows, without thinking of the dark of the night. Prejudices are anticipated judgments: we judge something or someone before its time, without having known the person or the situation adequately. So hasty judgments are used. They precede the experience, which reveals a lack of empirical data, incorrect or approximated judgments. The prejudice doesn't come into contact with the other person: it's just a way that our mind uses to face and solve some problems. Each one of us is a scrap, but belongs to the entire universe. Who suppresses his own authenticity kills himself and can't find the time to learn how to live.

Integration is not a problem that regards the different one, but every man as scrap. It's exactly starting from the limit that new and extra meanings for our life are born.

Often we would like to be different from what we are, without physical flaws, or stronger and braver in order to be able to win the difficult battles of life. And more, we would like to be sure to never be wrong, to not make ourselves eroded by doubts, pessimism and worries, to show ourselves always as secure people that never act wrong in public and never are attacked by anxiety while we do something and others are staring us. We learn to accept even our insecurity and we don't have to mix it up with the sense of our value. We must accept us as we are, only in this way we can accept others. We are not happy when our mind is conflict-free, but when we are able to accept them.

You see, by now children and kids like you

replace actors in advertisements of well known brands. The winning idea of this initiative is the normality message. Prejudices will disappear more and more: a lot of people like you have the right to express their abilities, to have the same opportunities as anyone else and can't be considered different and incapable to lead an autonomous life. Sometimes we assist to the most amazing events, someone has even been able to achieve a degree.

Diversity has to be always understood in order to knock down the preconceptions of disinformation and reach normality and inclusion.

Also, it's more and more spread between experts the idea that people with disabilities first of all need to find and cultivate what they have in common with all the others.

Social integration will happen slowly, starting from the family then in the school environment.

Parents, often, are called to "rethink" and restructure their own life for each one of their sons' growth. This requires time and energy.

That's why it's necessary the intervention and the help of the institutions, the services and the territory.

Sometimes, down children are involved in the game of rugby, a sport that equates them: the players feel part of a group with a common goal. Volunteers follow the child on the field, they try to talk to him and stimulate him, maybe when he tries to abstract himself. In this way barriers start to crumble.
You are stronger than what you think, because you transmit me the sense of life, that is purely the one of living. Each one of us is born with an intrinsic value: life.

And nobody can take it of us: neither failures, neither others' critiques. Even if we live in a society or in a group, we must realize that living in a community isn't easy. Often, difficulties to be faced rise, problems to be solved, contrarieties to be crossed, setbacks, misunderstandings . Each one of us lives in what he is, he exists, lives.
What can a person do to reduce other people's judgment? What does a person who thinks she is

not worth a dime? She does everything it's in her power to prove them that she's worth a lot, she's worth as they do or more than them. She tries to have more to be able to show it to others. But you never worry about this. Neither your parents do because they gave you the light of life in the name of unconditioned love. And they don't care to identify the sense of your or their value in function of what other people will think. Your life perhaps will be better than the one of a lot of human beings that run, hurry, become neurotic in order to reach money, success, popularity and certainties that may collapse at any moment.

And they don't realize that their life wears out in this crazy running. You are able to joy of every little joy, of every gesture of affection and friendship. You know how to authentically behave and others can think whatever they want. You don't need to be false, to show them that you're worth.

Express what you are, right now, life doesn't wait.

Your authenticity is beautiful, it cancels the

fatigue to pretend, you can show your humanity. If you want, you can whistle in the street cheering up the ones who would like to do it but don't dare.

Authenticity makes you "feel" always in the best moment, it makes you feel lively, happy, it makes you fly.

In a precise moment of the life of the universe, between thousands of people, a unique and unrepeatable human being was born: you.

You represent something original, exclusive.

It never existed, and never will someone who is the same as you are. You have ways to perceive, to listen and see that are only yours. Life isn't life if it isn't experimented in the originality of our own feeling, in the freedom or our acting. You will never assume behaviors that don't belong to you, otherwise you will never be able to develop you potentialities. Your life will be more and more beautiful if you let you be yourself.

Many are the reasons that could make you not accept your individuality: the need for security, the need of company, the fear to be marginalized, the little will to fight to affirm your individuality and be respected. But you don't have to surrender, you have to fight together with those who love you to hope in an always better life.

Every heart crave for another heart with whom it can conjoin. Only love can give a sense to things.

Love is freedom and it grows in the measure in which each one finds the harmony in the diversity. Hope, so, becomes a dream that turns into reality: don't be afraid to live, be proud to exist.

In you there is something that people can't show and that, so, isn't easy to understand. When I stare at you silently, listening your sweet whispers and caressing your thoughts I realize that down syndrome is a geniality that we mere mortals aren't able to understand.

In our life, crises represent a danger but also a big opportunity. The solution for every problem, as far as it can be practical, has an its own spiritual quality. And the complexity of life, sometimes, doesn't allow simple answers. Helps have to be searched in different ways. The spiritual strength can help us use our latent potentiality. Don't be afraid of the present, you are surrounded by the love of your loved ones.

Don't be afraid of the future, you will be an artist and, as all the other artists, you will see the world with different eyes. How will you see others while you grow up? With the gaze of sweetness and love, because you don't care about prejudices. You only care about living. You won't know neither envy, neither competition.

Our gazes and eyes always follow the advices of the heart. Your heart is pure, the others are the ones that can learn from you. From you that, as a pure being, can see the gazes of the sky, can live the time and can love and can return to life its wings with the value of simplicity.

Our existence will never be an adventure with no return, but it's a voyage towards the future. We don't have to worry if we aren't able to win the Oscar of life, what is important is to be joyful in the moments we are living. Only this way every work we do will be a masterpiece. We can exist even with a few crumbs and we can love everything, despite not having anything. Who is able to appreciate the little he has got, has much; who isn't able to appreciate the much he has got, has little.

In your heart we can listen to the voice of the child that is in you and always will, like in each one of us. Your heart is big, it has an endless desire to know, to discover. You are outstanding when you marvel yourself in front of what you have just known. You often would dive in the new and you will want to get in the trains of life, unaware of where they are going. This is the amazing and fascinating aspect of our life! Life basically is a nice game: better to be children. Sometimes the worst risk is the risk that you do not run at all. Risk, risking you will open new horizons, often do what you can, what your desire of new pushes you to do. And you will be able to go through the one thousand unknown wonders, infinite roads of life without needing maps, guides and road signs.

YOU WON'T FEEL ALONE

By now a lot of things are changing, a lot of associations made by true angels will think of you and will stay next to you, in addition to the precious pearls of your life that are your father, your mother and all your loved ones.

While we are walking towards the sun we are never alone, even if nearly every one of us depends on someone, in order to go away from the sense of existential loneliness and insecurity. Actually we are never lonely people in the world and in the universe, we only have to find the courage to recognize ourselves as the grains of sand that build the dwellings of the beaches and the stars of the firmament.

You are a part of this universe and if you are here it means the universe needs you, his presence reflects in yours, even if in the face of his immensity you may feel lost and small.

You will meet who will help you to make your dreams grow. And you, like all the children, will grow up happy if you will receive messages of joy and caresses of hope, just like the tree that becomes greener and greener dodging bad weather because a lot of light surrounds it.

And you will be like the big tree that hugs the earth with its roots and caresses the sky with its branches.

And I wish you will always be able to meet a lot of light sources that will give you company, love, safety… that can understand you, appreciate you, love you and help you facing the little and the big difficulties of life.

Slowly, you will be able to give yourself all the happiness you desire. You will learn to joy listening to the silence in a wood, to caress the wind with your hands, you will smile listening to a symphony. You will be able to live peacefully, to be joyful for the essential without craving the unnecessary.

Our fear to be wrong, or worst to be bad judged by others is such to make us nip it in the bud the most creative and beautiful thoughts. Perhaps we don't go throught a lot of trouble to take some note and examine various solutions starting from our idea. Actually every idea, at the beginning, it's just an idea and it needs to be developed and extended even in a different direction from the one we expected. A great number of discoveries was made, moreover, as a result of an error.

In every person exist positive aspects that have to be cultivated. Work on this aspect supporting its developing, doesn't mean close the eyes in front of the rest, but it means that it's needed to valorize at most every single emerging potentiality.

It's always needed to evaluate different possibilities, different ways of examining a determined event. After all, what we already know, rather than give us security, can sometimes lead us into gross errors. Isn't this the way in which various car accidents happen?

If every time that someone expresses an expected and "well-known" judgment we put ourselves in the position of who see things from another angle, we could discover many original, creative, and positive solutions. In our journey we can often run into storms, in every corner of the world. But you know, my dear child, that no storm will last forever, something will change. In every desert we will be able to run into fresh oasis and geniality often rises from stress, from the need to dare the fate that sometimes seems to be inclement. Hope doesn't leave us on the ragged edge and will give to all of us and to your heart the desire to go on and keep on living.

While you are walking towards the sun always look but don't be afraid to see, because beyond the blurred vision there are a lot of vivid colours for you. After all, a rose with no thorns doesn't exist. Thorns belong to every life form. The thorny bushes stand on the shores of beautiful islands, contrasting the white and pure color of the fine sand. It does not matter if the petals of the rose fade quickly, while its thorns last long: new buds and new roses will be born for you.

THE FUTURE

The value of life is limitless, any disadvantage, any damage is always a precious little thing in connection with it.

You are far away from most of the insatiable human beings' characteristics and you will be in wonder every day of "living". The new day is yours, it belongs to you, no one can take it away from you.

Don't be afraid of the future, you are a son of God and He won't abandon you. You too will feel the warm and enchanting perfumes of life. Everything changes on the earth, everything evolves, everything transforms.

Our future is the faith, the future is GOD.

"Every place on earth

is the horizon of my eyes.

from one point to another of the universe

our recalls

are the eco of the voice itself.

No one is a stranger to me

Between these distances.

My roots are in the center of the Earth."

WALKING TOWARDS THE SUN

The meeting with the little Filippo procures the writer the occasion to treat a very actual issue in the contemporary society: the diversity created by disability. However, it is read in terms of opportunity and not of disadvantage, according to the inclusive perspective that has developed in the academic environment in Italy in recent decades. Today it's enough just enter any class of primary school to see that children with Special Educative Needs related to disability, disorder or difficulty of learning have increased compared to the past; so for this reason it's asked firstly to the school but also to the entire society to change their own way of thinking about disability regarding at it no more as abnormal, but rather accepting it. We are talking about the creation of an inclusive society, that is able to accept the diversity of the disabled and welcome them in their uniqueness, trying to develop at most their capacities.

What seems an ideal vision can become every day more real if every one of us does his best in doing his part.

Where to start? Maybe spending some time with some of these children and with their families would help a lot of people to understand what is understood when we are talking about "special" needs or "different abilities". Staying in contact with them we can observe all the critical situation these people bump into, but also all the diligence, joy, love, desire of living that characterize them and their loved ones.

The book develops in this sense, wishing for the little Filippo (and for extension for every child like him) to find, along his walk of life, people able to help him in his difficult journey to develop his "sane part", the one that leads to building up competences and autonomy. The writer imagines that the little Filippo and his family are "hardly walking towards the sun", this may bring defeats and dark times, but definitely will be able to create joy, love and light.

Silvia Spadoni

Index

Traduzione in lingua inglese a cura di:

Giulia Mauri

www.ingramcontent.com/pod-product-compliance
Lightning Source LLC
Chambersburg PA
CBHW070835310526
45788CB00017B/1118